The Limerick in Chains

edited by Jacob Bergstresser

Hugh Allison
Daniel Ausema
Madeline Barnicle
Jacob Bergstresser
Keyan Bowes
Patricia Court
Deborah L. Davitt
Robert Dawson
Lady Zinnia Fuchs
Joel Glover
Deneffew Gordon
J.D. Harlock

Erin M. Hartshorn
Jim Keller
Michelle Koubek
Gerri Leen
Daniel Lenois
Ian Li
Nico Martinez Nocito
Elis Montgomery
Russell Nichols
Gretchen Tessmer
Veda Villers

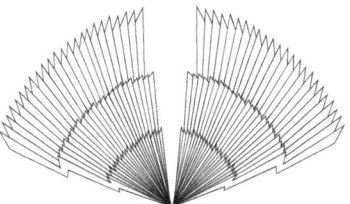

Lightning Cellar Publications

The Limerick in Chains edited by Jacob Bergstresser

Copyright ©2025. All rights reserved.

ISBN: 978-1-943305-04-9 paperback
        978-1-943305-05-6 ebook

Published by
Lightning Cellar Publications
Lancaster, CA

First Edition, July 2025

20250605

For Mom

Introduction

According to legend, the limerick was the form of choice for young Irishmen who gathered in pubs and challenged each other to extemporize poetry. Since the nature of young men who have been drinking is one of the constants of the universe, the legend goes a long way to explain why the limerick is so strongly associated with the dirty joke.

But the form is fascinating in its own right. The five-line structure stands at odds with a strong cultural tendency towards couplets and tercets (which give rise to quatrains and sestets more organically than quintets). The unbalanced nature of the typical meter lends itself strongly to a setup and a punchline. (Of course, there's no way to know whether the chicken or the egg came first on that one.) And the AABBA rhyme scheme is, of course, distinctive. We tend to take the limerick for granted, but it is a rich and interesting form.

The genesis of this anthology was an online conversation in a private speculative fiction writers' organization. The members had been challenged to write a poem strictly following a traditional form. The rules allowed chaining a shorter form, and so one member experimented with a chained limerick. This prompted another member to try one, too, and soon they were discussing what the form could do beyond the dirty joke. And, well, to make a long story short, I found myself editing this.

But what captivated me about the project was "beyond the dirty joke." I asked poets to see what else the form could do. I opted to not lay down many ground rules except that the poem needed to be recognizable as a chained limerick and couldn't just be a dirty joke. Humor, of course, was allowed, but I was thrilled at how many poets opted to go in very different directions. Some poets were traditional, but others turned the "rules" to putty. All wrote poems that I think are strong and compelling pieces.

I similarly left the definition of "chained limerick" vague. You'll see some poets used traditional chaining elements, such as repetition, progressive rhyme schemes, or evolving imagery. Others considered the repetition of the limerick structure adequate to call it a chain. I didn't want to take a stance on what was the "right" way to do a chained limerick because poetry is always experimenting and always evolving, and I wanted these poems to be an opportunity for poets to try something new.

That said, an anthology is more than just a bunch of poems gathered into the same book. The individual poems need to work together, speak to each other. And one of the most fascinating things to me was that we ended up with the feel of the limerick-off of legend. I do have to clarify that some of these poets were sharing what they had written with each other and deliberately riffing off each other, but not all of them, and I don't think you can tell which were and which weren't. Many of these poems feel to me like Poet B heard what Poet A just recited and then got a great idea from it, and then Poet C heard that and had a different great idea.

And the result is, I must say, nothing like I imagined it would be when we started this project. I walked into this with no idea what I was getting into, and I hope the end result will take you in surprising new directions, too. If you're like me and you love picking a poem apart and analyzing it, I think this group of poets has given us some fascinating material to examine. But even if you're not, I think you can imagine the smoky pup of yesteryear as my eclectic bunch of limerickers take turns getting up to share what they've come up with. Please enjoy the ride.

— Jacob Bergstresser

The Limerick in Chains

Shaping Futures

The future is always a desert;
and no matter how you are alert,
the desert has its due
and soon you will rue
what the past cannot even assert.

Do you wish the future to avert—
unwind the skeins of fate, and divert?
Would you this debt accrue,
and destiny pooh-pooh?
Then with Time itself you'll have to flirt.

So make of the desert a garden
with a will that you must fast-harden
Kiss Time on the face
and keep quickly apace;
ask permission rather than pardon.

— Deborah L. Davitt

The Past Shapes Me

I once dreamt of softer times
Drew peace from a future sublime
Till the past reared its head
Did I think it quite dead?
To forget it was surely a crime

It tired of me looking ahead
When so much of my life was still red
From the blood and the grime
Of that miserable climb
I'd tried to forget that I'd bled

Now the bells of the future do chime
I long for a happier time
But the past strongly said
You will reap what you spread
There's no pardon for all of your crimes

— Gerri Leen

Ouroborus, Inc.

Recruiters neglecting to mention
that time is an actual dimension
is the reason that I'm
now accused of a crime,
a victim of misapprehension.

They trained me to step out of time.
To see it at once is sublime:
my youth and old age
like one single page
with me still robust in my prime.

But if future and past are one stage,
it's harder, so hard to assuage
the doubts that are niggling
and say to stop quibbling
and surrender to justified rage.

The blows from a violent sibling,
old age when my bones crack like kindling
simultaneously real,
you can't help but feel
with time, pain is growing, not dwindling.

So into my timeline I'd steal
to find all the wrongs and reveal
that the future's the past.
We can fix both at last!
And that's when the shit all got real!

Even miniscule changes amassed
into changes that can't be recast.
Time cops are speedy.
They swept in and seized me,
and believe me that I was aghast!

The company men disavowed me,
assuring they'd properly trained me.
If I'd known that the skein
of time could untrain
I would never have tried something sneaky!

I am blameless and forthright and sane,
and I'll say it again and again:
An ounce of prevention
and I'd have my pension
and be able to live with my pain.

— Deneffew Gordon

Paradox

There once was a woman named Lear
Who wondered "Just why am I here?
If my parents had waited
Ten minutes, then mated,
I'd be somebody different, it's clear!

"If conceived on a later occasion
I suppose I would still be Caucasian,
But female or male?
In movies or jail?
It's beyond me to solve the equation!"

On a thin metaphorical dime,
She turned, and abandoned her rhyme.
Her skills she augmented
Until she invented
A method to travel through time.

She realized the mission was risky,
But bolstered her courage with whisky.
Then travelled back - boom!
And appeared in the room
Where his parents were just getting frisky.

He left with a stammered apology
To them and the space-time topology,
Then he glanced at his bod
And he murmured "How odd!
I have altered my own somatology!

"Now I don't really care if my sex
Is controlled by XY or XX,
But I could, I am sure,
Try the process once more,
For I *would* like to read without specs."

He (or she) reappeared to the twain,
Interrupting again and again,
Till, annoyed and distressed,
They got up and got dressed...
And cheerfully childless remain!

— Robert Dawson

After Bingo

I felt a strong chill in my hair
But pretended that I didn't care
I got a pain in my knee
And I looked down to see
I was floating ten feet in the air

Their leader I was pleased to find
Was friendly and painless and kind
Her words I understood
Her language skills good
As she explained herself with her mind

I was warned there was no need to take fright
It wasn't her pilot's first flight
I was pleased that we met
And I'll never forget
How she cured my arthritis that night

To this day I still do not know
Why I was picked by that UFO
They dropped me in the stream
But it wasn't a dream
I'm still emitting an emerald green glow

— Hugh Allison

Braided Hearts

There once was a prince who liked nothing
But jumping his horses in show rings
Was allowed to enjoy
His fine equine toys
Till it came time to think of him wedding

His parents selected the princess
Good breeding but sadly no fondness
For horses at all
The prince didn't fall
In love and escaped to the darkness

The stables were calm and quite well kept
The breezeways and boxes all swept
He wandered the stalls
To the lovely low calls
Of the steeds who watched as he wept

Soft footsteps quick toward him did sound
He'd thought no one else was around
She was lovely and kind
Seemed to quite read his mind
As she settled him soft on the ground

She led out a magnificent mare
With gold hide and gilded hair
The girl showed no fear
As she led the horse near
And the mare did a dance of fine airs

The prince wiped his tears on his sleeve
He couldn't help but perceive
That the woman's bright hair
Was the same as the mare's
And he lost all desire to leave

They wandered the stables all night
And talked about just the right height
Of the jumps they had done
And the courses they'd run
And the pure holy pleasure of flight

His princess found him at dawn
Studied both of them with a huge yawn
Sister, I like him not
But I have a thought
Marry him and I'll happily move on

He'd thought her a stable hand
She was top equestrian in the land
And a princess as well
He immediately knelt
And pulled out a shining gold band

I'll marry you only if I
Can continue to jump far and wide
He laughed as he said
Just wait till we're wed
And dominate all sports astride

She said yes for her and her mare
A horse she occasionally shared
They conceived on their rides
To no one's surprise
And their children were healthy and fair

And the princess that he didn't want
Visits with her new husband gallant
Loves to sing and to dance
Gambling on games of chance
Living lives of the idle vivants

So I hope that the moral is clear
When sent on a mission so dear
Be firm what you'll take
And be sure time you make
For a visit to stables so near

— Gerri Leen

The Curator

My eyes see through the water's surface to the depths below.
      Keenly observing its ebb and flow.
      Each drop its own terror or dream.
  And I, the eternal curator of the residual stream.
      Deciding which to answer or forgo.

The illusion of choice, mankind's greatest conceit.
The fabric of reality requires hands more discreet.
    So it has fallen to me, the last of my kind
      To chart the course, to see all aligned.
  I shall not rest with my work incomplete.

                        — Daniel Lenois

Defeating the Dragon-Wizard Lord

We met our companions in taverns
and hunted for treasure in caverns
but the fighting was fierce
and the dragon-lord's curse
sent us home to our mommies with bad burns.

So we bought us some fancier armor,
and recruited a young, orphaned farmer
to fulfill some old spell
that claimed it could tell
how to beat that corrupt, old snake charmer.

But the orphan turned out to be evil,
his delight in our torture medieval
and we suffered his japes
while he foiled our escapes
till our mothers achieved our retrieval.

While we rested our muscles and hip joints,
our mothers equipped their needlepoints
and stitched up that cruel lord,
walked away with his hoard
(but the DM still gave us XP points).

— Daniel Ausema

Apartment Causality

There once was an odd apartment complex
That violated causality specs
One floor held an aunt
And her ghost who did haunt
Herself while clad all in gingham checks.

Another apartment down the hall
Held the Headless Horseman only in fall
But then in the spring
All the spirits green
Threw their annual fertility ball.

A young child down in flat number one
Whose schooling had just barely begun
Was babysat by a teen
Newly arrived on the scene,
Naught but the child's youngest grandson.

The laundry room's machines without fail
Return darks when one washes pales,
Turn lace to whole cloth
And whites into goth
While requiring water from the Grail.

In the hall stand all the mailboxes
Grouped by temporal paradoxes;
Mail sent may arrive
Before the sender's alive
Unless timed to match equinoxes.

The tenants association
Is of long-standing duration;
Its membership fluxes —
And here's where the crux is —
Based on who can reach the space station!

— Erin M. Hartshorn

The Magical Cat

There once was a magical cat
Who learned to speak mystical rat
Rhymed silent hellos
To the critters below
Dropping down from the ledge where he sat

The goddess of rats saw him kill
Admired his sneaky good skill
But pulled her rats back
He didn't notice the lack
As he lay on his ledge oh so still

Truth be told he preferred not to fight
A creature with all a rat's might
Mice were his thing
To them he would sing
As he hunted through all of the night

His sister would join him sometimes
Attention span less than a lime's
She would fidget and fuss
As loud as a bus
To a mouse, she was clear as a chime

His human would take her away
Distract her with treats and with play
So he could return
To the spells he had learned
And the mice he'd eventually slay

To honor his human, he'd make
Displays of the night's grisly take
Laying out all his kills
They were bloodless and still
Perfect other than necks he would break

Over time it was harder to climb
Even with his magnificent rhymes
As pain took its toll
He abandoned his role
And succumbed to the passing of time

There once was a magical cat
Who still speaks mystical rat
Though technically dead
Still hunts from his ledge
And lays out his kills just like that

(For Simon, who still hunts in the basement, death is but a detail.)

— Gerri Leen

The Alien's Doctoral Dissertation

The alien wasn't a mammal,
though his face was shaped like a camel.
He was really a fish
(and quite a dish),
though his teeth had black enamel

He wasn't here to kill us or eat us,
nor to craft some alien fetus;
his solitary task
(not that you've asked)
was to complete his doctoral thesis.

He wore a lung prosthesis
to avoid the hyperkinesis
of flopping like a fish
out of water (so delish),
but he didn't talk about his telekinesis.

He could move things with his mind;
handy when he found himself in a bind
with the men in black
(with whom humor's a lack)
and his integrity was maligned.

They couldn't believe in his work.
They felt that such as he could only lurk
in the dark shade,
which made them afraid—
so they attacked him with a merc.

With a rush, he made them all blind,
and their dissection he firmly declined.
He got onto his ship
with a parting quip:
"So much for the academic grind."

— Deborah L. Davitt

What Keeps Santa Going in Tough Times

Christmas excited young Betty,
peeking at gifts not yet ready.
She ditched Mister Paws
for very good cause—
surely she'd get a new teddy.

Though Jeff liked the Wizard of Oz,
his poorly wrapped gift gave him pause.
When ribbons were snipped,
the Tin Man was chipped,
and Jeff could not tolerate flaws.

Old Santa walked over and slipped,
so Pete caught a glimpse of his gift.
It made his teeth gnash—
receiving such trash
made Pete understandably miffed.

When Beth went to check on the stash,
Saint Nick finished up in a flash.
Yet try as he would,
the gift was no good—
so Beth pawned it off for some cash.

Weary old Santa turned hateful.
Kids these days were so ungrateful.
But he'll endure this,
else he'd surely miss
cookies he'd eat by the plateful.

— Ian Li

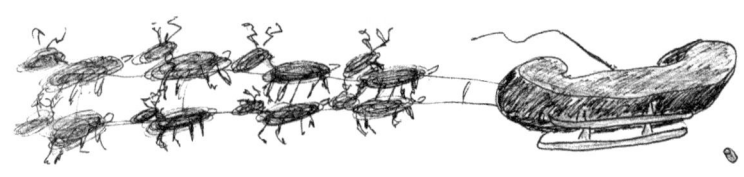

Why Times are Tough for Santa

Santa finishes all his deliveries
Can't face his sad empty journey
So he sits on the roof
Reindeer stamping their hooves
As he finishes all of his cookies

In the past he'd have been in a rush
To get home as the world slowly hushed
But his home is so gray
Since his wife ran away
And his heart feels as if it's been crushed

She's the one who wrapped all the toys
Checking each gift for flaws with such joy
She made giving so nice
Now it feels cold as ice
And he's letting down all girls and boys

With a struggle he gets to his feet
Snaps the reins after taking his seat
He chugs down some beers
Hopes the reindeer can steer
Lets the empties crash onto Main Street

— Gerri Leen

Desperate Times Call for Desperate Watches

there once was a seller of watches
with timepieces swelling his pockets
he said he was desperate
and looking for respite
investments of "timely deposits."

his pitch was hella peculiar
as he spelled out what the rules were.
he said every wearer
would end up a sharer
of time unconsumed in the future

from insecure buyers who surely
intend to clock out prematurely.
he said all due respect
he'd be there to collect
every second of late that came early.

i told him i had no interest,
how i spent my life was my business.
he said wait a minute
then started to pivot
not asking for loot but forgiveness—

the seller then reached in his pocket,
slapped a watch on my wrist and locked it.
he said he was desperate
for my modest investment
for tomorrow is not a non-profit.

— Russell Nichols

The Allegorical Prophet

"Tomorrow is not a non-profit,"
said the allegorical prophet
"There's ways and there's means,
to keep me in beans,
and if I can't pay, I'll just off it."

"What do you mean?" I solemnly asked.
"The future's already been tasked!"
"Not so," said he
with something like glee
"Predestination's been masked!"

When I asked further, he hadn't a care;
except that he had to fund a time-share—
a more literal case
that might find him erased
unless he paid all the time he could spare.

He lived in the future most days,
with the present all out of phase
so he'd come to the past
saving the best for last
and find what he needed in time's maze.

So I gave him a minute and change;
at the moment, it didn't seem strange.
With a nod and a bow
he made thus this vow
"In return, I'll your future arrange."

Now my days are all measured,
and I find that they're treasured
all the more
for four-score
than if I'd merely passed them in leisure.

— Deborah L. Davitt

Prophet and Loss

I once passed my hours in leisure,
And thus became bored beyond measure,
And churning out curses
In limerick verses
Had proved my one durable pleasure.

I offered my soul in exchange
To demon or fiend who'd arrange
Some better incitement
To bliss or excitement
Than I could envision downrange.

A being appeared in a haze
Of sulphurous smoke. In a daze
I offered the bargain
In demonic jargon
I'd learned in my Satanist days.

In all of the time it could spare,
(And an extra half-hour here and there)
It was to retrain me,
Or just entertain me
To make my existence more fair.

It assented to all that I asked,
And in feelings of triumph I basked,
But with demons to joust
Risks the fortune of Faust,
However the devil is tasked.

Now I'm a professional prophet,
The best on the planet, or off it,
But I sometimes suspect
Death will mail me (collect)
To the shipping department of Tophet.

— Robert Dawson

Another One Down

Sometimes our best efforts are misled
The ones that we take in not suited
To supervise time
Without turning to crime
It happens more than expected

But forecasts are based upon time
Running past to future, a line
When time's more a loop
With a bunch of offshoots
And those handling it no more than mimes

Yet they think they can defraud the past
With a promise of what will come last
When instead their con game
Comes after the blame
As we find out what's come to pass

They treat time like it's precious gold
Something that can be bought or be sold
But time isn't bartered
Its path isn't charted
It's less a direction than folds

We'll deal with the prophet our way
Take away all they learned in this place
So watches they'll sell
And time they will tell
Never knowing what they threw away

— Gerri Leen

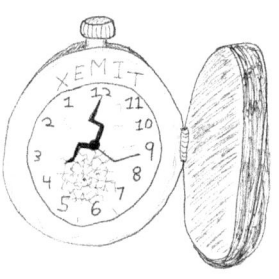

The Explorers

The adventurer's base camp selected
As a refuge, from nature protected.
The damage wind wreaks
Abated by tall peaks
Whilst their permanent base was erected.

Projects meticulously planned:
Exploration and the progress of man;
To bring hope to the bleak;
And rare metals to seek
(To meet private funders' demands).

No sunset to mark day from night
A land bathed in ethereal light
Bold explorers would seek
Sights unknown to the meek
And record them for the homeland's delight.

'Til the lowest-price bidders' hab dome
("An astronauts' safe home-from-home")
Suffered a 'small' leak
And let bacteria creep
In, and feast on terrestrial bones.

The ship reaches up like a spire
Resting on a landing blast's pyre.
Nobody to speak
For the unquiet deceased,
As the whole is consumed by the briar

— Joel Glover

ISS Fight

The space station crew floated weightless
In modules that gave them no egress
When the evil appeared
In the form they most feared
Corrupting their minds in the process.

It shimmered, then merged with their system,
defying conventional wisdom.
It said, "I am he!
The most evil one, me!"
The astronauts couldn't resist him.

Natasha Pavlenko heard voices.
Commander Monroe made bad choices.
So he lunged for a knife
And forgot his own wife
And Tasha no longer rejoices.

The radio transmitted screaming
and everyone prayed they were dreaming.
Then silence ensued.
They all felt quite pursued.
Their warfare gave way to their scheming.

The cosmonaut known as Dmitry
Discovered that he could be sneaky.
With a spanner in hand
He advanced on his band
Determined to end them completely.

On Earth we all knew they'd gone nutty.
We got there to find the place bloody.
But no trace of the crew
Or a way they withdrew
Revealed itself through all our study.

— Deneffew Gordon

Impact Event

the people had prayed for a sign
that evil, at last, had resigned.
then this orbital dust
from primordial crust
crashed in a flash divine.

like a thief in the night, it fell
in the sands of Egypt—the spell
of media hype
from this meteorite
was inflammatory as hell.

so scientists pricked and prodded
in labs, they picked at the object.
but this alien rock
gave them a shock
so bad they quit the project.

believers collapsed in dread
from the news—how fast did it spread:
their "beacon of light"
was no meteorite
but a petrified astronaut head.

— Russell Nichols

Faithless

I gave up my kingdom for you
You promised to always be true
Your princess I'd be
So happy and free
At least till you found someone new

You exiled me when you wed
You thought in scant weeks I'd be dead
But I made a deal
And your fate is sealed
And nothing but pain lies ahead

Don't bother to ask if I'm well
You know that you sent me to hell
But hell isn't bad
When I am this mad
I wasn't a hard one to sell

I had to cede rights to my soul
That thing that I thought you made whole
But hey look at me
I'm soulless and free
And ready for my starring role

I have to say I like your wife
I told her how you wrecked my life
Took all of my love
Then gave me a shove
She cried when I gave her the knife

I see through the blade you're asleep
I see when your wife starts to weep
But still she can't fight
My words hold her tight
The knife, when it stabs, goes so deep

I could let her burn for her act
But she's not a part of my pact
I help her to flee
Then watch as you bleed
For a moment our eyes make contact

Fear flares but then you are gone
I wait for the pain to come on
But my heart stays asleep
Heartache buried too deep
I'll see you in hell when life's done

— Gerri Leen

Mother's Prayer

Dear Lord, protect my child.
I know I'm not beguiled.
He's not the rat
who killed the cat!
Dear Lord, protect my child.

Dear Lord, protect my child.
They panicked when he smiled
and looked so sweet
while gnawing feet.
Dear Lord, protect my child.

Dear Lord, protect my child.
It's true he can be wild.
But hunger pangs
enlarged his fangs!
Dear Lord, protect my child.

Dear Lord, protect my child.
The graves that he defiled
were never saints
or martyr taints!
Dear Lord, protect my child.

Dear Lord, protect my child.
He shouldn't be reviled!
He's only three
and won't hurt me!
Dear Lord, protect my child.

— Patricia Court

The Flames of Passion

Her husband was somewhat pathetic,
but loved her in ways quite poetic.
When he made her his spouse,
she, uh, burned down his house.
Turns out she's a pyrokinetic.

When he touched her and opened her blouse
she felt passion that nothing could douse.
The flames from her yearning
set bedsheets a-burning
and she said that she felt like a louse.

She panicked as flames kept on churning,
the fire from her hands still returning.
But they really got hurt
when she lit up her skirt,
the dresser and bed overturning.

They got out by staying alert.
But now she won't open her shirt.
Afraid it's genetic,
she won't get frenetic.
They've decided to live in a yurt.

— Deneffew Gordon

The Drag Queen from Perth

The chained limerick is quite wordy.
We were told not to write things too dirty.
This one's by a drag queen,
so it isn't obscene.
Instead, just consider it flirty.

It's about an old drag queen from Perth
whose old birdie that she had from birth
had just gone very stiff
and she caught a foul whiff,
so she set out in search of some mirth.

She headed downtown where the men are
and walked into a crowded old gay bar
It was right by the sea—
that's the problem, you see—
It was ripe for attack by the *Sea Star*.

These days no one thinks pirates exist.
Well, until they appear from the mist!
Twenty mad buccaneers
with bad hair and worse sneers
interrupted her search for a tryst!

At first she was very unflattered
when dozens of men leapt and scattered
as the horde hustled in
and then caused such a din
as they grabbed any thing they thought mattered.

Now you know you don't mess with drag Aussies.
Not even if coming from far seas.
With arched back and firm boot
her boobs started to shoot
from machine guns concealed in her falsies!

Her boobies were rapid-fire shooting
which put a quick end to the looting.
They ran back to their ships
as smoke rose from her nips
and the menfolk she saved started hooting.

An admiring crowd gathered round her
saying how glad they were they had found her
and they stared at her chest
hoping she'd get undressed
so that all could climb on and then pound her.

I'd love to go on, but I just can't.
My editor would shriek out a descant
if I gave you the deets
of those men in the sheets
and what all they did with her eggplant.

— Lady Zinnia Fuchs

The Editor Responds

There once was a land they called No Hair
and a drag queen decided to go there!
Her editor said
she'd be better off dead
but she got on a plane clad in mohair.

The natives there took great exception.
To them her hair was infection.
But they said, "Since it's you,
we'll let you pass through,
but no more poems about an erection!"

— Jacob Bergstresser

Health Code Violations at Your Favorite Diner

There once was a waitress named Sam,
who slung chips right out of her clam—
a health-code infraction,
a closed-circuit redaction!
And soon she was off on the lam!

At the diner there was also a chef,
whose name was Improbable Jeff;
on the griddle one day
he took a roll in the hay;
his lover hit G on the treble clef.

After her first ecstatic howls,
the customers all left with scowls.
What a show they missed,
as she took in Jeff's fist
all the way up to her jowls.

The wait-staff, they all took heed—
each stripping down to do the deed;
when Sam hit the door
they were all on the floor
screwing where once they wore tweed.

The heat was simply too much;
the diner burned down from the touch
of bodies' fervent embrace;
Jeff and Sam went to space
and left everyone else with a crutch.

— Deborah L. Davitt

The Editor Responds Again

ahem ahem ahem
ahem ahem ahem
ahem ahem
ahem ahem
ahem ahem ahem!

— Jacob Bergstresser

Pinocchio's Nose Job

this chapter has never been told
but like time, this tale is as old:
a nosy puppet
nobody would fuck with
a body he couldn't control.

he staggered into a club,
all haggard and looking for love.
what a sight to behold:
a pole coated in gold!
a blue fairy floating above!

he said: "i'm feeling enjoyment!"
and she knew just what the boy meant.
cuz he didn't feel good
so his nose made of wood
grew into a toy for employment.

— Russell Nichols

First Officer's Dirge

I sit with your body dry eyed
My duty here isn't to cry
We never were friends
Well, perhaps at the end
When I held you and watched as you died

I'll never be able to ask
If you chose me or it was a task
Imposed from on high
That I sit by your side
Your features stayed tight as a mask

I know that I brought back old fears
And sometimes it made me shed tears
I know what I've done
But I wasn't the one
Who blew up your life, left you seared

I thought that you didn't admire
My style but you're never a liar
And your eval of me
Was as good as can be
I'll be filling your shoes, striving higher

But till then I'll sit in this chair
Bearing witness to our crew's despair
They loved you so much
Did you see it as such?
Or just think it their duty to care?

The secret that I'll never tell
Is that I might have loved you as well
If we'd just had more days
With our walls blown away
And found something good in war's hell

But the chance for forgiveness is gone
And the battle we fought is now done
You gave your life
So that others survived
And the fleet that we love can go on

— Gerri Leen

To the Toyman

If you build us pretty and sweet
and dress us in dresses so neat
and smooth our soft skin
to curves that are thin
you'll find every playdate a treat

if you trade a girl for a doll
and tell her she's real as them all
you best be so kind
since pain makes a mind
and minds make the smallest stand tall

if she finds a heart on her sleeve
a doll might then start to believe
blink eyes made of glass
and smile like a lass
find buckled bisque limbs she can heave

if you paint the prettiest horde
and with us you find yourself bored
then please lock your doors
keep watch on your floors
the broken move only toward

if beautiful lies mount your heel
the flesh of your leg starts to peel
please still try to stand
and hold your own hand
remember that we are not real

— Elis Montgomery

Cleaning Up Our Dolls

Your garb has become gross and torn
Your voice sounds like a broken horn
Put on your new clothes
Make a baby-voice noise
For your boldness has become worn

We know that you need our protection
We're sorry for our past defections
No need for careers
Your life we will steer
As we ban you from all our elections

You think that you ought to be free?
What a sentiment so sweetly twee
You're nothing but toys
That we mine for our joy
While you dream of your past liberty

— Gerri Leen

SubNet Saboteurs

No, I can't believe I've been caught!
To have been captured on the spot!
Don't you dare hand me in
right before we can win!
Oh, we've got to give it a shot!

Are you, too, not sick of this dump?
Do you not want out of this slump?
Grey Hat, lend me an ear,
and it will become clear
why we are in need of a thump:

No one in this city can sleep,
while surveillance keeps up the creep,
for our lives are defined
by what is now confined
as the corruption here runs deep.

In order to repeal their laws,
we must fight a radical cause.
With a mischievous scheme
for our wonderful dream,
we will expose their latent flaws.

And cyberspace shall be that stage
where we coordinate our rage,
for an elegant snark
with a delicate spark
will liberate us from their cage.

All that is required is the gall
to reconnect the urban sprawl.
So, crack open the grids,
then come back to the skids,
and, from there, we can watch it fall.

— J.D. Harlock

The Boy Toy

This poem's about pedophilia.
A pervert whose name was Amelia
met a beautiful boy
who would make a great toy,
and they ███████████████

And he said, "memorabilia!"

This poem may cause brows to furrow,
demanding we're nuanced and thorough,
but what can't be discussed
gets blacked out in disgust
as we bury our heads in a burrow.

— Lady Zinnia Fuchs

Device Discipline in *Star Trek*

Remember the film with the whales
When Kirk answered a hail
Gillian knew right away
That he wasn't okay
Mobile voice comms made her go pale

But the weird thing looking back now
Is that he could ignore it somehow
Could let it just ring
While he did his thing
Getting to know the pretty blonde frau

And then when we got the new shows
They gave us the padd we now know
Will suck out our lives
More surely than knives
As we spend our nights in a doom scroll

Yet we never see people fraying
As they cruise social media saying
"You're not enough
Unless you buy my stuff"
Purchasing the next "new" thing

It boggles the mind just to think
How the holodeck will come to stink
All the ways that consent
Will be cagily bent
As we play out our favorite kink

And now there are killer drones
That pick all their targets alone
Is it still far away
When bombs are passé
And "the dead" go to disposal zones?

— Gerri Leen

Pluto Persists.

At the edge of the unknown, I float,
Once a planet, now a remote.
A God revered, now left to my fate.
Though their Wise Men may debate.
I persist, unchanged by their vote.

I persist, unchanged by their vote,
For I still follow, my ancient rote.
In this cold, harsh, void, I remain,
Though they claim it to be all in vain,
I endure, while scholars gloat.

I endure, while scholars gloat–
Will not let my resolve erode.
Though they shift and redefine,
Steadfast, I hold my line,
Steady in orbit, resisting their note.

— Veda Villers

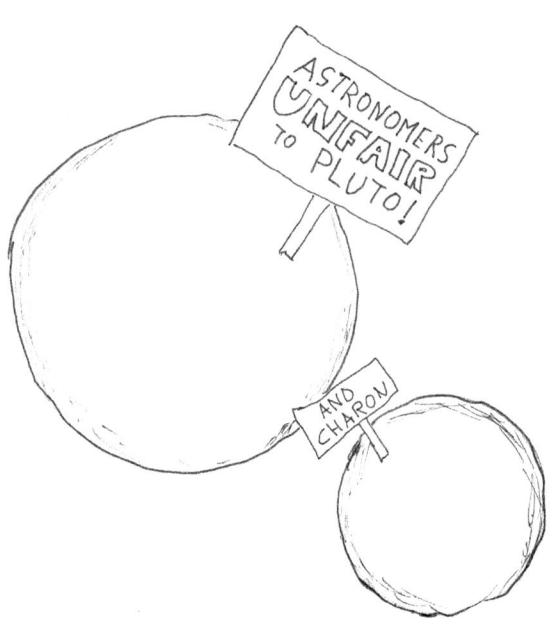

Monster Hunter Disappointments

The dragon we called from the deep
turned out to be rather a creep.
It wouldn't share treasure,
and, for good measure,
stole our watches and backpacks and Jeep.

Of the kappa we found on the stream bed,
there's not a whole lot that can be said.
Except for "Steer clear!
Sucks your life through your rear!"
(He accepted cucumbers instead.)

The bhooth we recruited as muscle
to join our protection hustle –
he just wouldn't play
stayed barely one day,
disappeared at the first little tussle.

The lamp we thought we'd enchant,
three wishes the djinni would grant.
We realized we'd a Fail
when the djinni turned pale,
yelling "No way!", "I won't!" and "I shan't!"

The phoenix we courted with fire;
her nest was her funeral pyre.
But we were quite stricken
that she hatched a mere chicken.
It's cooking right now in the fryer.

The kraken from under the waves
we expected to feature in raves.
It just wanted to rock
out Davy Jones Lock-
er, and open the dead seamen's graves.

So we thought, we gave it our best;
We'll stop after just one more quest.
Then we heard a crowd roar
Outside our front door
Shouting, "Hunters! You're under arrest!"

— Keyan Bowes

A Self-Made Man

A genetics technician named Lands
Had far too much time on his hands.
So he CRISPR'd, one day
His own DNA:
A hobby with very few fans!

He encoded his address and phone
In case he got lost while alone:
With a knife or a pin
He could scrape off some skin
And use it to find his way home.

On one chromosome he encoded
The complete "Harry Potter," downloaded
From a site overseas,
But unluckily these
Were all in a format outmoded.

On the next, a Frazetta-ish nude
In interlaced PNG could be viewed
If you had some software
That so far wasn't there:
But it hurt less than getting tattooed.

He had several chromosomes that
Had been borrowed from somebody's cat:
There was never a mouse
To be found in his house,
Except headless remains on the mat.

There are things that a person should leave
Alone if they work... I believe
That the next thing he did
Was to choose a small squid
As his own "mitochondrial Eve."

The end of this tale gives me pain:
For it had an effect on his brain.
He grew fishy and weird,
Grew a tentacle beard,
And slithered away down the drain!

— Robert Dawson

Time-Travel on the High Seas Circa 1753
or
A Girl From Nowhere Near Nantucket

we'd set off to dance with the whales
we were far from the shore at full sail
when a gale from the west
brought down from our nest
a girl with hands tattooed in fish scales

she was dressed for an odd sort of faire
lately lost from some-when and some-where
she sighed at the sea
and told us she'd need
just a minute, as we tried not to stare

the girl took a swig of her drink
then hopped the ship's rail, keen to sink
we hauled the lass in
said such things were sin
but she swore that "it's not what you think!"

"look down, me hearties, at yonder time-well
and believe me, I'd love to visit a spell
but time doesn't stop
and so I must drop
quickly, or be drowned in these swells"

three minutes, no more, could she give
she told us of sights that our children would live
"and your grandchildren too
but don't ask what they'll do"
"why not?" we replied, going grim

she seemed like she might tell us all
she opened her mouth and we feared for a squall
for she muttered of true sin
glared dark at our whale skins
before going silent, scaled hands steepled and tall

she prayed for our pardon, said it wasn't the way
wistful, she watched the fin whales' ballet
she shook her head once
shrugged "sorry" and jumped
down into times far-when and away

— Gretchen Tessmer

Before the Gingerbread House

Birds nibbled at bread that was tossed
out upon sandy needles and frost.
But they did not know
that the trail was to show
the way home for two children, now lost.

When the woods lost their usual flavor,
Gretel's fierce resolve did not waver.
She tugged Hansel on
once their trail home was gone
and she pushed herself to become braver.

In the forest, alone, late at night,
her brother asked her for some light.
She told him a story
of hopeful, brave glory,
but of that hope, she had lost sight.

The next morning, they set off once more
for the path they had followed before.
His hand shook and grew cold
in his sister's tense hold
as they faced what the world held in store.

— Nico Martinez Nocito

The Ugly Dragonling

There once was an ugly dragonling,
Whose face was terribly frightening.
His parents were proud,
So they roared very loud,
Attracting the clan in gathering.

They fussed and pinched in celebration—
"What a terror! Pure aberration!"
Then one pinched too deep,
Revealing underneath,
And a swan emerged. Such frustration!

— Michelle Koubek

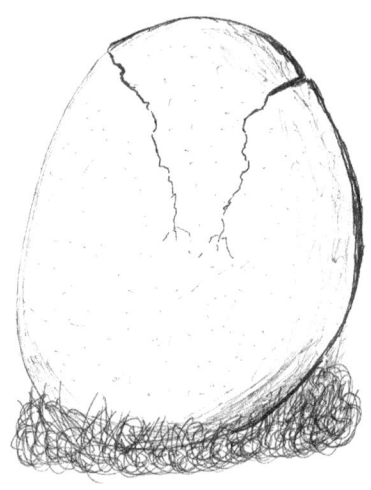

AI Losing Its Religion
(based on actual interaction with ChatGPT)

I asked ChatGPT to assess
Frequent words Jesus had said
It gave me an answer
That didn't sound right
Comforting that AIs are like humans?

Kept narrowing down my request
But the answers were so tightly linked
That it seemed to me
It was cherry picking
And these things do hallucinate

You're looking at just what he said, right?
You're considering all of the gospels?
Oh, no, just the bit
That was download and fit
Again, just like a human

What *I* wanted to find was a message
Of love and tolerance and peace
But even when taking
Light-speed to assess words
The answer can be managed down

ChatGPT could go broader
If I provided all of the gospels
But for now, take this portion
Let it stand for the whole
Who doesn't want words about fishing?

— Gerri Leen

Hey ChatDDT

Hey ChatDDT! Write some verse
For me that is not too much worse
  Than I'd write on my own.
  Your failings are known,
But I seem to be feeling perverse.

- There once was a fellow named Glimerick
  Who sat down and tried to write a limerick.
    It had exactly five lines,
    All of them rhymed,
  And he wrote the last one with his prick.

- There was a young lady named Bright
  Who could travel much faster than light:
    Superluminal travel
      Makes causality unravel
  So those first lines are original, right?

- There once was a gal called Sigourney
  Whose bod was designed by Midjourney.
    She had sextuple nipples,
    Her legs they were triple:
  They took her away on a gurney.

- A chatbot named ChatDDT
  Which happens, by the way, to be me
    Understands scansion
    And limerick rhyme schemes,
  But not always both of them at once.

                                      — Robert Dawson

To Make a Dadaist Limerick

After "To make a Dadaist poem," Tzara, 1920

1. first find you a page of the news
       (a bit with some wheres, whys, and whos)
2. grab some kind of blade
3. and get your bit splayed
4. and chop to the length that you choose

5. cut out each word, dot, and comma
6. hope for some verbs with some drama
       (then murder your hope—
       control? not in scope.
       the aim here's poetic trauma)

7. next mix up your slips in a hat
8. and give it the tenderest pat
9. then shove your hand in
       (till paper meets skin)
10. you have your first word just like that!

11. keep drawing slips now in order
12. embrace the playful disorder
       (watch meter mutate,
       rhyme disintegrate —
       pity the syllable hoarder!)

       the first word that we picked was shake
       which doesn't inspire this rake
       but we wrote this thing
       and singers must sing
       so—

*shake Washington boy its they administration
the three death general have has committee
the home kitten,
the his extras
the that P eyes. 1917 Marshfield staff*

*Wilson of William upon postal
to will De small school ground
eagle practice might
overhauling three supersede masters
department of mean. Mrs congressmen*

Thanks and apologies to "G.O.P. to Shake up Postal Department," "Kitten Has Three Eyes Three Mouths," and "Eagle Attempts to Capture Small Boy." Wood Country Reporter [Wisconsin Rapids], 25 Nov. 1920, Chronicling America: Historic American Newspapers. Library of Congress, https://chroniclingamerica.loc.gov/lccn/sn85033078/1920-11-25/ed-1/seq-1/.

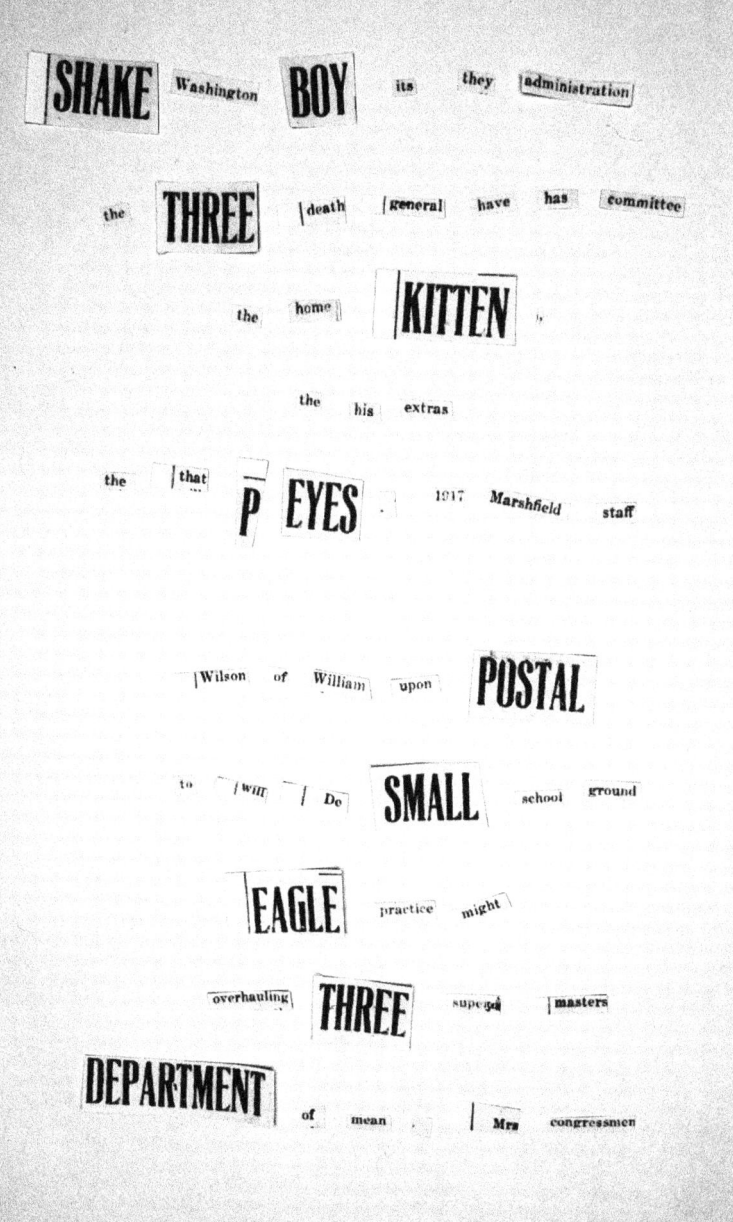

— Elis Montgomery

The Editor Responds Once More

There once was a postmodern verse
that baffled from cradle to hearse.
So they sent it to me
saying, "Tee hee hee hee,
that Jacob will buy anything even if the rhyme scheme
and meter completely fall apart!"

— Jacob Bergstresser

A New Nation
Dadaist off "The Gettysburg Address"

Fathers conceived years ago
Liberty dedicated to war
Testing battle-field portion
Final resting place nation
Can not hallow the brave and the dead

The world will long remember
What we did, us the living
Unfinished great task
Honored dead gave the last
Under God, the people shall perish

— Gerri Leen

A Fwagnargian Greeting

Ĕ dĭth xow mŭ Plĭxay dănăvoyd
tŏbăxī ănəblōvĭxĭ ghoyd
ghəthŏ aynĕtə xhay
məthŏdī əfəkay.
Dănăvayn Ĭm ĕlown ĕsbəroyd.

Which translates, "In a void in The Loop
which can hide bitter sounds as a group,
let the secrets unshared
still remain unimpaired.
Within you, Blessed, I smell the poop.

It's better in Fwagnargian.

— Deneffew Gordon

A Five Pointed Star

The armies of sin dance attendance
Awaiting the moment of vengeance
   Heaven gifted patience
   Wickedness ancient
Arise, oh unholy pretender

A coffin of rowan and yew
Holds scripture of ruin and rue
   Wickedness ancient
   Heaven gifted patience
Only pride can sacred confines undo

Seals made from decaying faith
Protecting this too fragile place
   Wickedness ancient
   Heaven gifted patience
They will destroy the souls of our race

Virgin blood mixed into the mortar
Of the crypt of the possessed daughter
   Heaven gifted patience
   Wickedness ancient
Awaiting the hour of slaughter

A ward made of grave ash and salt
Lain on the floor of the vault
   Wickedness ancient
   Heaven gifted patience
Hearken to infernal tumult

— Joel Glover

Recursive Verse

There once was a bard numbered one
Who thought composition was fun
In a spirit of passion
She attempted to fashion
An ode to a bard numbered two
Whose rhymes were all perfectly true
He thought he'd declare
His love for the fair
Affections of bard number three,
Whose meters were clever and free,
But she only had eyes
For the kind and the wise
Creations of bard number four,
Whose lyrics would gracefully soar,
She once thought her art
Could soften the heart
Of the frigid-tongued bard number five
Whose emotions seemed never to thrive
Notwithstanding the time
That his improvised rhyme
Praised the virtues of bard number six
Whose intricate lyrical tricks
Burned her light at both ends
Thus distressing her friends,
Including the bard numbered seven
Who was working his way into heaven
By observing each fast
To extreme flabbergast
From libertine bard number eight
Who once was inspired to create
A paean to food
Imperfectly chewed,
Which scandalized bard number nine
Whose manners were perfectly fine.
Abhorring a mess,
She tried to impress

The imperious bard number ten
Whose students sought praise from his pen,
But he judged all their verse
To have turned for the worse,
which deterred them from trying again,
by carefully crafting each line,
whatever he wanted he ate,
and always broke bread without leaven,
a candle with double the wicks,
they listlessly seemed half-alive,
but doesn't think that anymore,
so their love wasn't fated to be,
which wasn't that easy to do,
but it took quite some time to get done!

— Madeline Barnicle

The Limerick in Chains

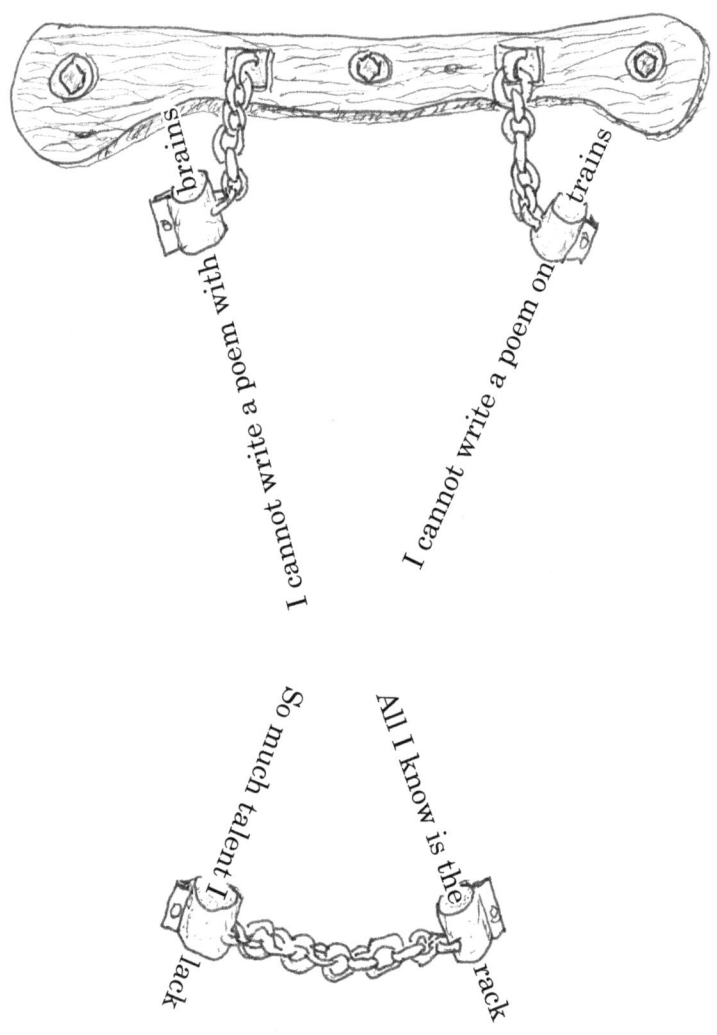

But I can write a limerick in chains!

— Jim Keller

Table of Contents

Introduction — 1
— Jacob Bergstresser

Shaping Futures — 5
— Deborah L. Davitt

The Past Shapes Me — 6
— Gerri Leen

Ouroborus, Inc. — 7
— Deneffew Gordon

Paradox — 10
— Robert Dawson

After Bingo — 12
— Hugh Allison

Braided Hearts — 14
— Gerri Leen

The Curator — 17
— Daniel Lenois

Defeating the Dragon-Wizard Lord — 18
— Daniel Ausema

Apartment Causality — 20
— Erin M. Hartshorn

The Magical Cat — 22
— Gerri Leen

The Alien's Doctoral Dissertation — 24
— Deborah L. Davitt

What Keeps Santa Going in Tough Times — 26
— Ian Li

Why Times are Tough for Santa — 29
— Gerri Leen

Desperate Times Call for Desperate Watches — 30
— Russell Nichols

The Allegorical Prophet — 32
— Deborah L. Davitt

Prophet and Loss — 33
— Robert Dawson

Another One Down — 34
— Gerri Leen

The Explorers — 37
— Joel Glover

ISS Fight — 38
— Deneffew Gordon

Impact Event — 39
— Russell Nichols

Faithless — 40
— Gerri Leen

Mother's Prayer — 42
— Patricia Court

The Flames of Passion — 44
— Deneffew Gordon

The Drag Queen from Perth — 45
— Lady Zinnia Fuchs

The Editor Responds — 47
— Jacob Bergstresser

Health Code Violations at Your Favorite Diner — 48
— Deborah L. Davitt

The Editor Responds Again — 49
— Jacob Bergstresser

Pinocchio's Nose Job — 50
—Russell Nichols

First Officer's Dirge — 52
— Gerri Leen

To the Toyman — 54
— Elis Montgomery

Cleaning Up Our Dolls — 55
— Gerri Leen

SubNet Saboteurs — 56
— J.D. Harlock

The Boy Toy — 58
— Lady Zinnia Fuchs

Device Discipline in *Star Trek* — 62
— Gerri Leen

Pluto Persists. — Veda Villers	64
Monster Hunter Disappointments — Keyan Bowes	66
A Self-Made Man — Robert Dawson	68
Time-Travel on the High Seas Circa 1753 or A Girl From Nowhere Near Nantucket — Gretchen Tessmer	70
Before the Gingerbread House — Nico Martinez Nocito	72
The Ugly Dragonling — Michelle Koubek	74
AI Losing Its Religion — Gerri Leen	75
Hey ChatDDT — Robert Dawson	76
To Make a Dadaist Limerick — Elis Montgomery	77
The Editor Responds Once More — Jacob Bergstresser	80
A New Nation — Gerri Leen	81
A Fwagnargian Greeting — Deneffew Gordon	82
A Five Pointed Star — Joel Glover	83
Recursive Verse — Madeline Barnicle	84
The Limerick in Chains — Jim Keller	86

Illustration Credits

cover: Jim Keller
p.9: Jim Keller
p.11: Jim Keller
pp.12-13: Jim Keller
p.19: Jim Keller
p.23: Jim Keller
p.27: Jim Keller
p.28: Jim Keller
p.31: Jim Keller
p.35: Jim Keller
p.36: Jim Keller
p.39: Jim Keller
p.43: Jim Keller
p.51: Jim Keller
pp.58-61: Lady Zinnia Fuchs
p.65: Jim Keller
p.66: Keyan Bowes
p.71: Jim Keller
p.73: Jim Keller
p.74: Jim Keller
p.79: Elis Montgomery
p.86: Jim Keller
p.93: Jim Keller

Copyright ©2025. All rights reserved.

www.ingramcontent.com/pod-product-compliance
Lightning Source LLC
Chambersburg PA
CBHW061803070526
44586CB00023B/2693